SEAFOOD

It is hard to believe that fish and shellfish were once so cheap that they were known as poor man's meat. In fact in 18th century England, oysters cost so little that it was not uncommon for them to be fed to cats!

Although today seafood is rather more expensive, it should be part of our everyday diet. In this book you will find recipes and ideas that are suitable for everyday family meals as well as for entertaining and special occasions. For those watching kilojoules (calories) and fat, the recipes in the Light Meals chapter will be particularly appealing.

THE PANTRY SHELF
Unless otherwise stated, the following ingredients used in this book are:
Cream   Double, suitable for whipping
Flour   White flour, plain or standard
Sugar   White sugar

WHAT'S IN A TABLESPOON?
NEW ZEALAND
1 tablespoon =
15 mL OR 3 teaspoons
UNITED KINGDOM
1 tablespoon =
15 mL OR 3 teaspoons
AUSTRALIA
1 tablespoon =
20 mL OR 4 teaspoons
The recipes in this book were tested in Australia where a 20 mL tablespoon is standard. All measures are level.

The tablespoon in the New Zealand and United Kingdom sets of measuring spoons is 15 mL. In many recipes this difference will not matter. For recipes using baking powder, gelatine, bicarbonate of soda, small quantities of flour and cornflour, simply add another teaspoon for each tablespoon specified.

CONTENTS

SOUPS

The variety of fish soups is almost limitless; they range from classic bisques to substantial bouillabaisses. As the cooking time for fish is so quick, fish soups are among the fastest of all soups to prepare, making them ideal for last-minute entertaining.

Bouillabaisse

BOUILLABAISSE

2 tablespoons olive oil
3 onions, chopped
1 fennel bulb, thinly sliced
4 cloves garlic, crushed
4 cups/1 litre/$1^3/4$ pt chicken stock
440 g/14 oz canned tomato purée
2 x 440 g/14 oz canned tomatoes,
undrained and mashed
1 tablespoon chopped fresh thyme
or 1 teaspoon dried thyme
2 bay leaves
$^1/2$ teaspoon ground turmeric
750 g/$1^1/2$ lb firm white fish fillets, cut
into 5 cm/2 in pieces
500 g/1 lb uncooked prawns, shelled
and deveined, tails left intact
4 uncooked crabs, halved
500 g/1 lb mussels, scrubbed and
beards removed
3 tablespoons chopped fresh basil
freshly ground black pepper

1   Heat oil in a large saucepan, add onions, fennel and garlic and stir over a medium heat for 5-6 minutes or until onions are soft. Stir in stock, tomato purée, tomatoes, thyme, bay leaves and turmeric, and bring to simmering.

2   Add fish, prawns, crabs and mussels and cook for 5 minutes or until seafood is just cooked. Discard any mussels that do not open after 5 minutes. Stir in basil and season to taste with black pepper. To serve, place seafood on a large serving platter and ladle soup into a tureen.

Serves 8

More of a stew than a soup, Bouillabaisse is one of the best known and most popular fish soups. It can be made using whatever seafood is available so use this recipe as a guide only. For a complete meal accompany the Bouillabaisse with crusty French bread and a glass of dry white wine.

ARTICHOKE AND PRAWN BISQUE

30 g/1 oz butter
1 onion, chopped
2 potatoes, chopped
440 g/14 oz canned artichoke hearts,
drained and chopped
3 cups/750 mL/$1^1/4$ pt milk
$^1/2$ teaspoon paprika
125 g/4 oz cooked prawns, shelled
freshly ground black pepper
1 tablespoon snipped fresh chives

1   Melt butter in a large saucepan, add onion and potatoes, and stir over a medium heat for 5 minutes or until onion is soft.

2   Add artichokes, milk and paprika and bring to the boil. Reduce heat to simmering, cover and simmer for 15-20 minutes or until potatoes are tender. Transfer soup to a food processor or blender and process until smooth. Return soup to a clean saucepan and bring to the boil.

3   Stir in prawns and season to taste with black pepper. To serve, ladle soup into bowls and sprinkle with chives.

Serves 4

This simple-to-prepare bisque with its creamy artichoke base makes the perfect starter for any dinner party. For an extra-special touch reserve a few of the prawns to use as garnish.

CREAMY MUSSEL SOUP

2¹/₂ cups/600 mL/1 pt dry white wine
1 teaspoon chilli paste (sambal oelek)
2 tablespoons lemon juice
2 cloves garlic, crushed
500 g/1 lb mussels, scrubbed and
beards removed
1¹/₂ cups/375 mL/12 fl oz cream
(double)
1 tablespoon chopped fresh dill
freshly ground black pepper

1   Place wine, chilli paste (sambal oelek), lemon juice and garlic in a large saucepan and bring to the boil. Add mussels and cook for 5 minutes or until shells open. Discard any unopened mussels. Using a slotted spoon remove mussels from liquid and set aside.

2   Strain liquid through a fine sieve and return to a clean pan. Stir cream into wine mixture and bring to the boil. Reduce heat and simmer for 10 minutes.

3   Remove mussel meat from shells and stir into soup mixture. Add dill and season to taste with black pepper. Serve immediately.

Serves 4

Remember, any mussels that do not open their shells after 5 minutes of cooking should be discarded; they are bad.

Tom Yam Gong

3 cups/750 mL/1^{1}/$_4$ pt fish stock
1 tablespoon chopped fresh lemon grass
or 1 teaspoon dried lemon grass
^{1}/$_2$ teaspoon finely grated lemon rind
2 tablespoons Thai fish sauce
250 g/8 oz button mushrooms, sliced
500 g/1 lb large uncooked prawns,
shelled and deveined
^{1}/$_3$ cup/90 mL/3 fl oz cream (double)
125 g/4 oz bean sprouts
2 spring onions, cut into
2 cm/^{3}/$_4$ in lengths
1 teaspoon chilli paste (sambal oelek)
^{1}/$_3$ cup/90 mL/3 fl oz lemon juice
3 tablespoons chopped fresh coriander
freshly ground black pepper

1   Place stock in a large saucepan and bring to the boil. Stir in lemon grass, lemon rind, fish sauce, mushrooms and prawns and cook for 3-4 minutes or until prawns change colour.

2   Reduce heat to low, stir in cream and cook for 2-3 minutes or until heated through.

3   Remove pan from heat, add bean sprouts, spring onions, chilli paste (sambal oelek), lemon juice, coriander and black pepper to taste. Serve immediately.

Serves 4

When making the stock for this soup, include the shells of the prawns to give a more intense flavour. See Techniques section for Fish Stock recipe. Chicken stock can be used in place of the fish stock if you wish.

STARTERS

Light, healthy and delicious, fish makes the ideal first course for any meal. Why not try Cheesy Grilled Mussels or Trout Ceviche as an elegant starter at your next dinner party? Or for pre-dinner nibbles, Curried Fish Parcels or Fish Knots with Lime Dip will fill the gap deliciously before the main meal.

Fish Knots with
Lime Dip

Fish in Radicchio
Leaves

Trout Ceviche

Calamari with
Curry Sauce

Curried Fish Parcels

Smoked Salmon Rolls

Anchovy Dip

Oysters with Caviar

Oysters Rockefeller

Creamy Oyster Dip

Octopus Cocktail

Cheesy Grilled Mussels

Fish Knots with Lime Dip

FISH KNOTS WITH LIME DIP

750 g/1^{1}/$_{2}$ lb firm white fish fillets, cut
into strips, each 1 x 7.5 cm/^{1}/$_{2}$ x 3 in
^{1}/$_{2}$ cup/60 g/2 oz dried breadcrumbs
2 teaspoons chopped fresh coriander
1 teaspoon finely grated lime rind
^{1}/$_{2}$ cup/125 mL/4 fl oz milk
^{1}/$_{2}$ cup/60 g/2 oz flour
1 egg, beaten
vegetable oil for deep-frying

LIME DIP
1 tablespoon hot fish or chicken stock
4 strands saffron
^{3}/$_{4}$ cup/185 mL/6 fl oz mayonnaise
^{1}/$_{4}$ teaspoon ground turmeric
1 tablespoon lime juice
freshly ground black pepper

1   Tie fish strips into single knots. Place breadcrumbs, coriander and lime rind in a small bowl and mix to combine. Dip each knot in milk, then in flour, egg and finally in breadcrumb mixture. Place knots on a plate lined with plastic food wrap, cover and chill for at least 30 minutes.

2   To make dip, place stock and saffron threads in a bowl and set aside to steep for 10 minutes. Strain stock mixture. Place stock mixture, mayonnaise, turmeric, lime juice and black pepper to taste in a bowl and mix to combine. Cover and chill until ready to serve.

3   Heat oil in a large, deep saucepan and cook knots in batches for 2-3 minutes or until golden. Using a slotted spoon remove knots and drain on absorbent kitchen paper. Serve with dip.

Makes approximately 20

When heating oil for deep-frying, check the temperature by dropping a cube of bread into the hot oil. The oil is at the right temperature when it will brown the bread cube in 50 seconds.
As saffron is a very expensive spice and is sometimes difficult to obtain, it can be omitted from this recipe if you wish.

FISH IN RADICCHIO LEAVES

250 g/8 oz firm white fish fillets,
skin and bones removed
1 teaspoon finely chopped
fresh coriander
^{1}/$_{2}$ teaspoon chilli paste (sambal oelek)
^{1}/$_{4}$ cup/60 mL/2 fl oz lime
or lemon juice
freshly ground black pepper
16 radicchio leaves

1   Chop fish into small pieces and place in a bowl. Add coriander, chilli paste (sambal oelek), lime or lemon juice and black pepper to taste and toss to combine.

2   Divide fish mixture into eight portions and wrap 2 radicchio leaves around each portion to form eight parcels. Carefully tie each parcel with cotton and place in a steamer.

3   Place steamer over a saucepan of simmering water, cover and steam for 8 minutes.

Serves 4

The radicchio makes this a very pretty starter, however you could use butter (round) lettuce leaves or spinach leaves for something different.

TROUT CEVICHE

This recipe is also delicious made with other fish. Choose any firm white fish fillets in place of the trout, or for something really special you might like to make the salad using fresh salmon.
To avoid the risk of food poisoning do not use shellfish such as prawns or mussels for this recipe.

500 g/1 lb trout fillets, skin and bones removed, flesh cut into bite-sized pieces
1 teaspoon finely grated lemon rind
3 tablespoons lemon juice
1 teaspoon finely grated lime rind
3 tablespoons lime juice
¹/2 cup/125 mL/4 fl oz dry vermouth
2 tablespoons finely chopped fresh dill
freshly ground black pepper
6 lettuce cups or lettuce leaves

1 Place trout, lemon rind, lemon juice, lime rind, lime juice, vermouth, dill and black pepper to taste in a bowl and toss to combine. Cover and refrigerate for at least 8 hours or overnight. Stir occasionally during marinating.

2 To serve, divide fish mixture between lettuce cups or line a salad bowl with lettuce leaves and top with fish mixture.

Serves 6

CALAMARI WITH CURRY SAUCE

500 g/1 lb calamari (squid) rings
¹/2 cup/60 g/2 oz cornflour
vegetable oil for deep-frying

CURRY SAUCE
1 tablespoon vegetable oil
1 small onion, finely chopped
2 cloves garlic, crushed
3 teaspoons curry powder
2 tablespoons plum sauce
2 teaspoons soy sauce
¹/2 cup/125 mL/4 fl oz water
1 tablespoon lemon juice
2 teaspoons brown sugar
2 tablespoons chopped fresh coriander
freshly ground black pepper

1 To make sauce, heat oil in a small saucepan and cook onion and garlic for 4-5 minutes or until onion is soft. Add curry powder and cook, stirring, for 1 minute longer. Stir in plum sauce, soy sauce, water, lemon juice and sugar, bring to simmering and cook, stirring occasionally, until sauce is reduced by half. Remove pan from heat and set aside to cool. Stir in coriander and season to taste with black pepper.

2 Toss calamari (squid) in cornflour. Heat oil in a large saucepan over a high heat and cook calamari (squid) a few at a time for 2-3 minutes or until lightly browned. Using a slotted spoon remove calamari (squid) and drain on absorbent kitchen paper. Serve immediately with sauce for dipping.

Serves 6

Either fresh or frozen calamari (squid) rings can be used for this dish. Freezing calamari (squid) has no adverse effect on it – in fact more often than not it tenderises it.

Trout Ceviche,
Calamari with Curry Sauce

CURRIED FISH PARCELS

20 long chives, blanched

CURRY CREPES
1 cup/125 g/4 oz flour
2 eggs
$^1/_2$ cup/125 mL/4 fl oz milk
$^1/_2$ cup/125 mL/4 fl oz water
2 teaspoons curry powder
1 teaspoon ground cumin
30 g/1 oz butter, melted

COCONUT FISH FILLING
1 tablespoon vegetable oil
1 clove garlic, crushed
1 small onion, finely chopped
1 teaspoon finely grated fresh ginger
185 g/6 oz firm white fish fillets,
cut into cubes
1 tablespoon desiccated coconut
1 tablespoon cream (double)
freshly ground black pepper

1 To make crêpes, place flour, eggs, milk, water, curry powder, cumin and butter in a food processor or blender and process for 1 minute. Set batter aside to stand for 1 hour.

2 Pour 1 tablespoon batter into a heated, lightly greased 18-19 cm/7-7$^1/_2$ in crêpe pan and cook over a medium heat for 30 seconds each side or until lightly browned. Remove crêpe from pan and repeat with remaining batter to make 20 crêpes.

3 To make filling, heat oil in a large frying pan and cook garlic, onion and ginger over a medium heat for 3-4 minutes or until onion is soft. Add fish, coconut and cream and cook, stirring, for 4-5 minutes or until fish is just cooked. Remove pan from heat and set aside to cool to room temperature. Place 2 teaspoons filling in the middle of each crêpe, gather up edges and tie with a chive to form a parcel or bag. Serve at room temperature.

Makes 20

The crêpes can be made in advance and frozen if you wish. To freeze, stack cold crêpes between sheets of greaseproof paper or freezer wrap and place in a sealed freezer bag, or wrap tightly in aluminium foil. Defrost crêpes at room temperature before using.

SMOKED SALMON ROLLS

20 slices smoked salmon
20 sprigs fresh dill

CREAM CHEESE FILLING
155 g/5 oz smoked salmon, chopped
3 tablespoons cream (double)
1 tablespoon lemon juice
1 tablespoon horseradish relish
250 g/8 oz cream cheese
freshly ground black pepper

1 To make filling, place smoked salmon, cream, lemon juice, horseradish relish, cream cheese and black pepper to taste in a food processor or blender and process until smooth.

2 Place 2 teaspoons filling along one side of each smoked salmon slice, then roll up to form a tube. Place rolls seam side down on a large serving platter and top each roll with a dill sprig.

Makes 20

These rolls are also delicious made with smoked trout instead of the smoked salmon. They can be made 2-3 hours ahead of serving and stored, covered, in the refrigerator until you are ready to serve them.

Curried Fish Parcels,
Smoked Salmon Rolls

ANCHOVY DIP

300 g/9¹/₂ oz sour cream or
natural yogurt
45 g/1¹/₂ oz canned anchovy fillets,
drained and mashed
3 tablespoons finely chopped dill pickles
freshly ground black pepper
2 teaspoons chopped capers

1 Place sour cream or yogurt, anchovy
fillets, dill pickles and black pepper to
taste in a food processor or blender and
process to combine.

2 Transfer dip to a bowl and garnish
with capers.

Serves 6-8

Served with cracker biscuits,
raw vegetable sticks or
Melba toast, this is one of the
easiest and tastiest starters
that you will ever make.

OYSTERS WITH CAVIAR

36 oysters on the shell
4 tablespoons black caviar or
lumpfish roe
fresh dill sprigs

HORSERADISH MAYONNAISE
2 tablespoons mayonnaise or sour cream
1 teaspoon lemon juice
1 teaspoon tomato paste (purée)
2 teaspoons horseradish relish
freshly ground black pepper

You may like to serve the mayonnaise separately and so allow each person to add their own if they wish.

1   Arrange oysters on a large serving platter and set the platter on a bed of ice.

2   To make Horseradish Mayonnaise, place mayonnaise or sour cream, lemon juice, tomato paste (purée), horseradish relish and black pepper to taste in a small bowl and mix to combine.

3   Top each oyster with a little mayonnaise, a little caviar, or lumpfish roe, and garnish with a dill sprig.

Makes 36

OYSTERS ROCKEFELLER

It is believed that this dish was created in the late 1800s at Antoine's, a well-known New Orleans restaurant. The name of the dish is said to have originated from a customer remarking that oysters prepared in this way were 'as rich as Rockefeller'.

36 oysters on the shell
500 g/1 lb spinach, chopped
1 cup/250 g/8 oz sour cream
2 cloves garlic, crushed
freshly ground black pepper
3 tablespoons finely grated tasty cheese
(mature Cheddar)
30 g/1 oz breadcrumbs, made from
stale bread

1   Remove oysters from shells and reserve both flesh and shells.

2   Boil, steam or microwave spinach until cooked, then drain well and place in a sieve. Using the back of a spoon, press spinach to remove as much moisture as possible.

3   Place sour cream, garlic and spinach in a bowl and mix to combine. Season to taste with black pepper. Place a teaspoon of spinach mixture in each oyster shell, then top with a reserved oyster. Top with another teaspoon of spinach mixture.

4   Place cheese and breadcrumbs in a small bowl and mix to combine. Sprinkle breadcrumb mixture over oysters and cook under a preheated grill for 3-4 minutes or until cheese melts and topping is browned.

Makes 36

Oysters with Caviar

Creamy Oyster Dip

CREAMY OYSTER DIP

$^1/_2$ cup/125 mL/4 fl oz cream (double)
$^1/_4$ cup/60 mL/2 fl oz milk
$^1/_2$ cup/125 g/4 oz sour cream
2 tablespoons tomato sauce
1 teaspoon cornflour
freshly ground black pepper
24 oysters, removed from shells, or 24
bottled oysters, drained

1   Place cream, milk, sour cream, tomato sauce, cornflour and black pepper to taste in a small saucepan and whisk to combine. Cook cream mixture over a low heat, stirring constantly, for 4-5 minutes or until mixture thickens.

2   Remove sauce from heat and stir in oysters. Serve immediately.

Serves 4

This dip is delicious served with Melba toast, crackers or thin slices of rye bread. To make Melba toast, cut bread into slices of a medium thickness and lightly toast. Cut crusts from toast and split each slice of toast horizontally. Cut each slice in half diagonally and bake at 180°C/350°F/Gas 4 for 5-7 minutes or until the edges curl and the toast is golden.

Right: Octopus Cocktail
Far right: Cheesy Grilled Mussels

To prepare octopus, remove gut by cutting off the head. To do this, hold the head firmly, then using a sharp knife cut through the flesh below the eyes (separating the head and tentacles). Place your index finger under the centre of the body and push the beak firmly up to remove. Discard head and beak. The tentacles can be cut into separate pieces or left on the body.

OCTOPUS COCKTAIL

2 cups/500 mL/16 fl oz water
$^1/_2$ cup/125 mL/4 fl oz lemon juice
1 teaspoon chilli paste (sambal oelek)
500 g/1 lb baby octopus, cleaned
1 lettuce, leaves separated

COCKTAIL SAUCE
$^1/_2$ cup/125 mL/4 fl oz tomato sauce
$^1/_4$ cup/60 mL/2 fl oz mayonnaise
$^1/_4$ teaspoon Tabasco sauce
freshly ground black pepper

1   Place water in a large saucepan and bring to the boil. Add lemon juice, chilli paste (sambal oelek) and octopus, and cook for 1 minute. Using a slotted spoon, remove octopus, place in a bowl, cover and chill.

2   To make sauce, place tomato sauce, mayonnaise, Tabasco sauce and black pepper to taste in a small bowl and mix to combine. Cover and chill until ready to serve.

3   Place a few lettuce leaves in each serving glass or dish, and top with octopus and a little sauce. Serve immediately.

Serves 4

CHEESY GRILLED MUSSELS

2 cups/500 mL/16 fl oz water
24 mussels, scrubbed and
beards removed

CHEESY TOPPING
2 cloves garlic, crushed
1 tablespoon finely chopped
fresh coriander
1 small red chilli, seeded
and chopped
1 teaspoon finely grated lemon rind
2 tablespoons grated Parmesan cheese
1 cup/60 g/2 oz breadcrumbs, made
from stale bread
60 g/2 oz butter, melted
freshly ground black pepper

1   Place water in a large saucepan and bring to the boil. Add mussels and cook for 5 minutes or until shells open. Discard any mussels that do not open after 5 minutes cooking. Using a slotted spoon remove mussels from liquid and set aside until cool enough to handle.

2   Remove top shells of mussels and discard. Loosen mussel meat in bottom shells and return meat to shells. Place shells on griller tray.

3   To make topping, place garlic, coriander, chilli, lemon rind, Parmesan cheese, breadcrumbs, butter and black pepper to taste in a bowl and mix to combine. Top each mussel with a little of the topping and cook under a preheated grill for 3 minutes or until mussels are heated through and topping is golden.

Makes 24

Mussels will live out of water for up to 7 days if treated correctly. To keep mussels alive, place them in a bucket, cover with a wet towel and top with ice. Store in a cool place and as the ice melts, drain off the water and replace the ice. It is important that the mussels do not sit in the water or they will drown.

LIGHT MEALS

*Fish is the perfect food for the health-conscious. In this section
you will find a selection of recipes ideal for weight watchers, for
those limiting cholesterol and fat intake and for those just
wanting tasty, healthy 'lite' recipes.*

Salmon Soufflés

SALMON SOUFFLES

220 g/7 oz canned red salmon,
drained and flaked
100 g/3½ oz bottled oysters, drained,
rinsed and chopped
2 teaspoons finely chopped capers
1 teaspoon finely chopped fresh dill
2-3 dashes Tabasco sauce
1 cup/250 g/8 oz low-fat cottage cheese
freshly ground black pepper
4 egg whites

1   Place salmon, oysters, capers, dill, Tabasco sauce, cottage cheese and black pepper to taste in a bowl and mix to combine.

2   Place egg whites in a separate bowl and beat until stiff peaks form. Fold egg white mixture gently into salmon mixture. Divide soufflé mixture between four lightly greased 1½ cup/375 mL/ 12 fl oz capacity soufflé dishes and bake for 30-35 minutes. Serve immediately.

Serves 4

Oven temperature
200°C, 400°F, Gas 6

At only 550 kilojoules (132 Calories) per serve, these soufflés make a wonderful main meal for any health-conscious cook. For a complete meal, serve with a tossed green salad and crusty wholemeal rolls.

FISH AND TOMATO GRATIN

500 g/1 lb firm white fish fillets, skin
and bones removed
60 g/2 oz grated tasty cheese
(mature Cheddar)
4 tomatoes, peeled and sliced
1 tablespoon finely chopped fresh
oregano or 1 teaspoon dried oregano
2 cloves garlic, finely chopped

1   Arrange half the fish fillets in a single layer in a lightly greased shallow ovenproof dish. Sprinkle with one-third of the cheese and top with half the tomato slices. Sprinkle with oregano and garlic.

2   Top with remaining fish fillets, sprinkle with half the remaining cheese and top with remaining tomatoes. Finally sprinkle with remaining cheese and bake for 30 minutes or until fish is cooked.

Serves 4

Oven temperature
180°C, 350°F, Gas 4

To lower the fat content of this dish even further, choose one of the low-fat cheeses in place of regular cheese when making this recipe.

SALMON WITH GINGER SAUCE

15 g/¹/₂ oz butter
2 x 155 g/5 oz salmon or ocean
trout cutlets
1 tablespoon finely sliced fresh ginger
2 tablespoons orange juice
1 tablespoon lime juice
1 tablespoon brown sugar
thin strips lime rind

Salmon is an oily fish which means that it has more Omega-3 fatty acids than white fish such as sole, plaice or whiting. Medical research has shown that Omega-3 has a lowering effect on blood pressure and blood fats.

1 Melt butter in a frying pan and cook cutlets for 3 minutes each side or until cooked. Remove cutlets from pan and set aside to keep warm.

2 Add ginger, orange juice, lime juice and sugar to pan and cook over a medium heat, stirring constantly, for 5 minutes or until sauce reduces and thickens slightly. Stir in lime rind. Serve sauce spooned over cutlets.

Serves 2

THAI-STYLE FISH FILLETS

Oven temperature
200°C, 400°F, Gas 6

4 x 155 g/5 oz firm white fish fillets
2 tablespoons lemon juice
freshly ground black pepper
1 tablespoon peanut (groundnut) oil
1 onion, finely chopped
4 tablespoons chopped fresh coriander
1 small red chilli, seeded and chopped

Any herbs of your choice may be used in this recipe. You might like to try basil, chives, parsley, thyme or rosemary or a mixture of herbs, depending on your taste and what is in season.

1 Arrange fish fillets in a single layer in a shallow glass, ceramic or stainless steel dish, sprinkle with lemon juice and season to taste with black pepper. Cover and set aside to marinate at room temperature for 30 minutes.

2 Heat oil in a nonstick frying pan and cook onion over a medium heat, stirring, for 4-5 minutes or until soft. Remove pan from heat and stir in coriander and chilli.

3 Cut four pieces of nonstick baking paper large enough to enclose each fish fillet. Place a fish fillet in the centre of each piece of baking paper, then top each fillet with one-quarter of the onion mixture. Fold paper around fillets to enclose and seal edges by rolling together firmly.

4 Place fish parcels in a shallow ovenproof dish and bake for 15-20 minutes or until fish flakes when tested with a fork.

Serves 4

Salmon with Ginger Sauce

CRUMBED FISH CUTLETS

4 x 155 g/5 oz white fish cutlets
2 tablespoons lime or lemon juice

HERB TOPPING
2 cups/125 g/4 oz wholemeal
breadcrumbs, made from stale bread
$^1/_2$ cup/45 g/1$^1/_2$ oz instant rolled oats
2 tablespoons finely chopped
fresh coriander
2 tablespoons snipped fresh chives
2 teaspoons olive oil
1 tablespoon vinegar
freshly ground black pepper

1 Brush cutlets with lime or lemon juice and cook under a preheated grill for 5 minutes on one side only.

2 To make topping, place breadcrumbs, rolled oats, coriander, chives, oil, vinegar and black pepper to taste in a bowl and mix to combine.

3 Turn fish and top each cutlet with one-quarter of the topping. Grill for 5 minutes longer or until fish is cooked and topping is golden.

Serves 4

Serve garnished with slices or wedges of lemon and accompany with new potatoes and a green salad.

TAGLIATELLE WITH TUNA

375 g/12 oz dried wholemeal tagliatelle
or spaghetti

TUNA SAUCE
1 onion, finely chopped
1 clove garlic, crushed
440 g/14 oz canned tomatoes, undrained
and mashed
1 tablespoon tomato paste (purée)
1 tablespoon dry red wine
2 zucchini (courgettes), sliced
440 g/14 oz canned tuna in springwater
or brine, drained and flaked
1 tablespoon finely shredded fresh basil
freshly ground black pepper

1 Cook pasta in boiling water in a large saucepan following packet directions. Drain, set aside and keep warm.

2 To make sauce, heat a nonstick frying pan and cook onion, garlic and 1 tablespoon of juice from tomatoes for 4-5 minutes or until onion is soft. Stir in tomatoes, tomato paste (purée), wine and zucchini (courgettes) and cook over a low heat for 5 minutes.

3 Add tuna, basil and black pepper to taste to pan and cook for 5 minutes longer or until heated through. To serve, place pasta on serving plates and spoon sauce over.

Serves 4

When using tuna and salmon canned in brine, drain off as much liquid as possible and add some cold water to the can. Drain off again and use fish as specified in the recipe. This removes over half the salt content and is handy when no-added-salt or salt-reduced products are unavailable.

Crumbed Fish Cutlets,
Tagliatelle with Tuna

CALAMARI IN TOMATO SAUCE

1 tablespoon olive oil
500 g/1 lb calamari (squid) rings
1 onion, chopped
3 cloves garlic, crushed
4 tomatoes, peeled and chopped
2 teaspoons chopped fresh marjoram or
$^1/_2$ teaspoon dried marjoram
1 bay leaf
1 cup/250 mL/8 fl oz red wine
freshly ground black pepper

1   Heat oil in a large saucepan, add calamari (squid) and cook over a high heat for 3-4 minutes or until browned. Reduce heat to medium, add onion and garlic and cook, stirring, for 3-4 minutes longer or until onion is soft.

2   Add tomatoes, marjoram and bay leaf to calamari (squid) mixture and cook, stirring, for 5 minutes.

3   Stir in wine, cover and simmer for 1 hour or until calamari (squid) is tender. Season to taste with black pepper.

Serves 4

When buying fresh calamari (squid) it should have a good colour, a slippery appearance and a fresh salty smell. Avoid calamari (squid) that have broken outer skins or those that are lying in a pool of ink.

PAELLA

One of the traditional dishes of Spain, paella varies from region to region and season to season. In Spain it is cooked in a large shallow paella dish; this ensures that the cooking liquid evaporates rapidly. A large frying pan will do the same job.

1 tablespoon olive oil
2 cloves garlic, crushed
1 onion, chopped
3 tomatoes, chopped
1 red pepper, chopped
1 teaspoon paprika
$^{1}/_{4}$ teaspoon saffron powder or ground turmeric
155 g/5 oz long grain white rice
3 cups/750 mL/1$^{1}/_{4}$ pt chicken stock
250 g/8 oz cooked chicken, chopped
125 g/4 oz fresh or frozen peas
250 g/8 oz small prawns, shelled
freshly ground black pepper

1   Heat oil in a large frying pan, add garlic, onion, tomatoes and red pepper and cook over a medium heat for 5 minutes or until onion is soft.

2   Stir in paprika, saffron or turmeric and rice and cook for 3 minutes. Pour stock over rice mixture and bring to the boil. Reduce heat and simmer for 10 minutes or until rice is almost cooked.

3   Stir in chicken, peas and prawns and cook for 5 minutes longer or until rice is tender and most of the liquid is absorbed. Serve immediately.

Serves 4

CRISPY BAKED FISH

750 g/1¹/₂ lb firm white fish fillets, cut
into 3 cm/1¹/₄ in squares
freshly ground black pepper
3 tablespoons safflower or sunflower oil
60 g/2 oz cornflakes, crushed
1 tablespoon lemon juice

1   Using absorbent kitchen paper, pat
fish dry. Place fish, black pepper to taste
and oil in a bowl and toss to coat.

2   Roll each fish piece in crushed
cornflakes and place in a single layer in a
lightly oiled shallow ovenproof dish.

3   Bake fish for 10-15 minutes or until
cooked. Just prior to serving, sprinkle fish
with lemon juice.

Serves 6

Oven temperature
200°C, 400°F, Gas 6

Using a fraction of the fat
that is normally required to
cook crumbed food, these
fish pieces are sure to be
popular with all those who
are watching their fat intake.
Whole fish fillets are also
delicious prepared this way.

TUNA PATE

200 g/6$^{1}/_{2}$ oz canned tuna in
springwater or brine, drained
1 small cucumber, peeled, seeded
and chopped
1 cup/250 mL/8 fl oz tomato juice
1$^{1}/_{2}$ tablespoons gelatine dissolved in $^{1}/_{2}$
cup/125 mL/4 fl oz hot water
1 tablespoon chopped fresh dill
1 teaspoon finely grated lemon rind
1 teaspoon lemon juice
2 teaspoons finely chopped capers
1 teaspoon horseradish relish
3 tablespoons low-fat natural yogurt
freshly ground black pepper

1   Place tuna, cucumber, tomato juice, gelatine mixture, dill, lemon rind, lemon juice, capers, horseradish relish and yogurt in a food processor or blender and process until smooth.

2   Season to taste with black pepper and spoon mixture into four individual dishes or jelly moulds. Cover and refrigerate for 2-3 hours or until firm.

Serves 4

At only 371 kilojoules (88 Calories) per serve, this pâté is the perfect first course for any dinner party. It also makes a delicious light lunch or supper dish when served with salad and crusty French bread or rolls.

SATAY SALMON PATTIES

440 g/14 oz canned red salmon,
drained and flaked
3 potatoes, cooked and mashed
2 tablespoons flour
1 clove garlic, crushed
1 teaspoon grated fresh ginger
1 teaspoon grated lemon rind
1 small red chilli, seeded and
finely chopped
2 teaspoons soy sauce
1 teaspoon curry paste (vindaloo)
pinch chilli powder
$^{1}/_{4}$ teaspoon ground cumin
2 tablespoons finely chopped unsalted
roasted peanuts
freshly ground black pepper
$^{1}/_{2}$ cup/60 g/2 oz sesame seeds
$^{1}/_{2}$ cup/60 g/2 oz dried breadcrumbs
1 tablespoon peanut (groundnut) oil

1   Place salmon, potatoes, flour, garlic, ginger, lemon rind, chilli, soy sauce, curry paste (vindaloo), chilli powder, cumin, peanuts and black pepper to taste in a large bowl and mix well to combine.

2   Place sesame seeds and breadcrumbs in a shallow dish and mix to combine. Shape salmon mixture into twelve patties and roll in sesame seed mixture. Place patties on a plate lined with plastic food wrap, cover and refrigerate for 30 minutes.

3   Heat oil in a nonstick frying pan and cook patties for 3-4 minutes each side or until golden and heated through. Remove patties from pan and drain on absorbent kitchen paper.

Serves 6

Kids will love these patties on a toasted bread roll with lettuce, tomato and cucumber.

Tuna Pâté,
Satay Salmon Patties

GRILLED CHILLI FILLETS

4 x 155 g/5 oz firm white fish fillets

CHILLI MARINADE
1 tablespoon vegetable oil
1 tablespoon Worcestershire sauce
1 teaspoon soy sauce
¹/4 teaspoon chilli powder
1 clove garlic, crushed
1-2 drops Tabasco sauce

1   Arrange fish fillets in a single layer in a glass, ceramic or stainless steel dish.

2   To make marinade, place oil, Worcestershire sauce, soy sauce, chilli powder, garlic and Tabasco sauce in small bowl and whisk to combine. Pour marinade over fish fillets and set aside to stand for 10 minutes.

3   Remove fish fillets from marinade and cook under a preheated grill for 2-3 minutes each side or until flesh flakes when tested with a fork.

Serves 4

When buying fish fillets, look for those that are shiny and firm with a pleasant sea smell. Avoid fillets that are dull, soft, discoloured or 'ooze' water when touched.

JOHN DORY ROLLS

Oven temperature
180°C, 350°F, Gas 4

$^{1}/_{4}$ cup/60 mL/2 fl oz lemon juice
2 cloves garlic, crushed
freshly ground black pepper
8 x 60-75 g/2-2$^{1}/_{2}$ oz John Dory fillets
16 spinach leaves, stems removed
1 tablespoon snipped fresh chives

LEMON SAUCE
2 tablespoons lemon juice
$^{1}/_{2}$ cup/125 mL/4 fl oz evaporated milk
2 teaspoons cornflour

1 Place lemon juice, garlic and black pepper to taste in a small bowl and whisk to combine. Brush each fillet with lemon juice mixture, then top with 2 spinach leaves, folding them to fit the fillets.

2 Roll up fillets and secure with wooden toothpicks. Place rolls in a lightly oiled, shallow ovenproof dish and bake for 20 minutes or until fish is cooked. Remove fish from dish, set aside and keep warm. Reserve cooking juices.

3 To make sauce, place the reserved cooking juices, lemon juice, evaporated milk, cornflour and black pepper to taste in a small saucepan and cook over a medium heat, stirring constantly, for 3-4 minutes or until sauce boils and thickens slightly. Spoon sauce over rolls, sprinkle with chives and serve immediately.

Serves 4

If evaporated skim milk is available, use it in this recipe to make a dish that is lower in kilojoules (calories).

SMOKED SALMON RISOTTO

1 tablespoon olive oil
2 onions, chopped
2 cloves garlic, crushed
$^{1}/_{4}$ teaspoon ground turmeric
315 g/10 oz short grain rice
1 red pepper, chopped
3 cups/750 mL/1$^{1}/_{4}$ pt fish or
chicken stock
3 spring onions, chopped
1 tablespoon chopped fresh basil
1 tablespoon snipped fresh chives
8 slices smoked salmon, cut into strips
freshly ground black pepper

1   Heat oil in a large nonstick frying pan, add onions, garlic and turmeric, and stir over a medium heat for 4-5 minutes or until onions start to soften.

2   Add rice and red pepper and cook, stirring, for 3 minutes longer. Add stock, bring to simmering and simmer, uncovered, for 20 minutes or until rice is tender.

3   Stir in spring onions, basil, chives, salmon and black pepper to taste. Serve immediately.

Serves 4

A risotto is a great one-dish meal. Accompanied by a tossed salad of mixed lettuces and herbs and a glass of dry white wine, this risotto is a delicious summer lunch dish.

MAIN MEALS

Fish is one of the healthiest main meal foods that you can eat and one of the quickest to cook. The recipes in this section range from simple rosemary-flavoured mackerel cutlets to a variation of a more exotic Japanese dish, Tuna Sukiyaki.

Fish and Vegetable Ragout

Fish and Vegetable Ragout

4 baby yellow squash or 2 zucchini
(courgettes), sliced
1 small head broccoli, broken
into florets
2 tablespoons olive oil
500 g/1 lb firm white fish fillets, cut
into large pieces
1 onion, sliced
$^1/_2$ red pepper, cut into strips
60 g/2 oz butter
$^1/_2$ cup/125 mL/4 fl oz dry white wine
$^1/_2$ cup/125 g/4 oz sour cream
freshly ground black pepper

1   Boil, steam or microwave squash or
zucchini (courgettes) and broccoli
separately until just tender. Drain and
refresh under cold running water.

2   Heat oil in a large frying pan and cook
fish over a medium heat for 1 minute each
side. Remove fish from pan and set aside.
Add onion and red pepper to pan and
cook for 2 minutes. Remove onion
mixture from pan and set aside.

3   Add butter, wine, sour cream and
black pepper to taste to pan, bring to the
boil and cook, stirring, for 4-5 minutes or
until mixture is reduced by one-third.
Strain sauce and return to a clean pan.

4   Stir squash or zucchini (courgettes),
broccoli, fish and onion mixture into
sauce and cook, stirring gently, for 3-4
minutes or until fish is cooked.

Serves 4

Any firm white fish fillets can
be used to make this tasty
ragout. You might like to
use other vegetables,
depending on what is in
season. Carrots, parsnips,
leeks and green pepper are
good choices for a winter
dish.

Fish with Rice Stuffing

1 x 1.5 kg/3 lb whole fish,
such as snapper or bream, cleaned
and skin scored
$^1/_2$ cup/125 mL/4 fl oz dry white wine

LEEK AND RICE STUFFING
185 g/6 oz rice
2 tablespoons olive oil
2 leeks, sliced
2 cloves garlic, crushed
3 tablespoons pine nuts
4 tablespoons sultanas
1 stalk celery, chopped
3 tablespoons chopped fresh parsley
1 teaspoon lemon juice
1 teaspoon finely grated lemon rind
freshly ground black pepper

1   To make stuffing, cook rice following
packet directions, then set aside. Heat oil
in a large frying pan and cook leeks and

garlic for 3-4 minutes or until leeks are
soft. Remove pan from heat and stir in
rice, pine nuts, sultanas, celery, parsley,
lemon juice, lemon rind and black pepper
to taste.

2   Fill cavity of fish with stuffing, close
cavity and secure with wooden skewers or
toothpicks. Place fish in a lightly greased,
shallow baking dish. Pour wine over fish
and bake for 35-40 minutes or until fish is
cooked. Baste 3-4 times during cooking.

3   Place fish on a serving platter, cover,
set aside and keep warm. Pour juices from
baking dish into a small saucepan, bring
to the boil and boil for 4-5 minutes or
until juices are reduced by half. Spoon
sauce over fish and serve immediately.

Serves 4

Oven temperature
180°C, 350°F, Gas 4

Whole fish cooks well in the
microwave – but remember
the eyes should be removed
before cooking as they can
explode.
To cook this dish in the
microwave, prepare fish and
stuffing as described in the
recipe, then place in a
shallow microwave-safe dish,
pour over wine, cover and
cook on MEDIUM-HIGH
(70%), allowing 5-6 minutes
per 500 g/1 lb of fish.

TROUT WRAPPED IN PROSCIUTTO

Oven temperature
180°C, 350°F, Gas 4

This simple way of preparing and cooking trout results in a deliciously fragrant fish which is moist and tender.

4 x 280 g/9 oz trout, cleaned and scaled
1 tablespoon olive oil
8 long slices prosciutto or lean ham
4 sprigs fresh thyme or rosemary

THYME MARINADE
$^1/_2$ cup/125 mL/4 fl oz olive oil
3 tablespoons lemon juice
2 cloves garlic, crushed
1 tablespoon chopped fresh thyme
or 1 teaspoon dried thyme
freshly ground black pepper

1 To make marinade, place oil, lemon juice, garlic, thyme and black pepper to taste in a small bowl and whisk to combine.

2 Place trout in a shallow glass, ceramic or stainless steel dish, pour marinade over, cover and refrigerate for 2 hours.

3 Cut four pieces of nonstick baking paper large enough to enclose each trout. Place 2 slices of prosciutto or ham side by side on each sheet of paper. Remove trout from marinade and place on prosciutto or ham. Place a sprig of thyme or rosemary in the cavity of each trout and wrap prosciutto or ham around trout. Spoon over remaining marinade and fold baking paper around trout to enclose. Seal edges by rolling together tightly.

4 Place parcels on a baking tray and bake for 20-25 minutes or until flesh flakes when tested with a fork.

Serves 4

ROSEMARY MACKEREL CUTLETS

Mackerel is an oily fish and so is high in Omega-3 fatty acids, making it ideal for anyone on a cholesterol-lowering diet. Omega-3 helps to lower blood pressure and reduce the fatty build-up on blood vessel walls. It has also been shown to reduce the tendency for the blood to clot and so lessens its 'stickiness'.

1 tablespoon olive oil
2 cloves garlic, crushed
4 x 155 g/5 oz mackerel cutlets or
thick fillets
3 tablespoons lemon juice
2 teaspoons fresh rosemary leaves or
$^1/_2$ teaspoon dried rosemary
freshly ground black pepper

1 Heat oil in a large nonstick frying pan and cook garlic for 1 minute. Add cutlets or fillets and cook for 3-4 minutes each side or until fish is browned.

2 Pour lemon juice over fish, sprinkle with rosemary and season to taste with black pepper. Cover and simmer for 5-8 minutes or until fish flakes when tested with a fork. Serve immediately.

Serves 4

Trout wrapped in Prosciutto,
Rosemary Mackerel Cutlets,
Fish with Rice Stuffing

WHITING WITH ORIENTAL RICE

Oven temperature
180°C, 350°F, Gas 4

If whiting is unavailable any firm white fish fillets or whole small fish could be used in its place. If using fish fillets the cooking time will be 10-15 minutes. The Oriental Rice is also delicious with pan-cooked or grilled tuna or swordfish.

4 small whole whiting, cleaned
and scaled
freshly ground black pepper
2 tablespoons olive oil
2 tablespoons lemon juice

ORIENTAL RICE
2 tablespoons olive oil
1 large onion, chopped
30 g/1 oz pine nuts
155 g/5 oz rice
1 tablespoon grated fresh ginger
$^{1}/_{2}$ red pepper, chopped
2 cups/500 mL/16 fl oz water
125 g/4 oz canned baby sweet corn
spears, drained and sliced
3 tablespoons sugar
2 tablespoons lemon juice
1 tablespoon chopped fresh parsley

1   Wash fish and pat dry with absorbent kitchen paper. Season cavity of each fish with black pepper to taste. Place oil and lemon juice in a small bowl and whisk to combine.

2   Cut four pieces of aluminium foil large enough to enclose each fish. Brush each fish with oil mixture and place one fish on each piece of foil. Fold foil around fish to enclose. Seal edges by rolling together tightly. Place fish parcels on a baking tray and cook for 20 minutes or until flesh flakes when tested with a fork.

3   For the rice, heat oil in a large frying pan and cook onion and pine nuts for 2 minutes. Add rice, ginger, red pepper and water. Bring to the boil, reduce heat and simmer for 15 minutes or until rice is tender and liquid has been absorbed.

4   Stir sweet corn, sugar and lemon juice into rice and cook for 2 minutes longer. Stir in parsley and season to taste with black pepper. To serve, divide rice between four serving plates, remove fish from foil and place on top of rice.

Serves 4

Right: Tuna Sukiyaki
This page: Whiting with Oriental Rice

Tuna Sukiyaki

2 tablespoons vegetable oil
3 small onions, quartered
6 small oyster mushrooms, sliced
185 g/6 oz bean sprouts
5 spinach leaves, stalks removed, shredded
1 red pepper, sliced
6 spring onions, cut into 2.5 cm/1 in lengths
250 g/8 oz tofu, cubed
440 g/14 oz canned tuna, drained and flaked
125 g/4 oz transparent noodles, rinsed in cold water
$^1/_2$ cup/125 mL/4 fl oz Japanese light soy sauce
1 tablespoon sugar

1 Heat 1 tablespoon oil in a large frying pan and stir-fry half the onions, mushrooms, bean sprouts, spinach, red pepper, spring onions, tofu, tuna and noodles over a high heat for 4-5 minutes.

2 Place soy sauce and sugar in a small bowl and whisk to combine. Pour half the soy sauce mixture over the tuna mixture and toss to combine. Serve immediately. Repeat with remaining ingredients.

Serves 4

Sukiyaki is traditionally cooked quickly in small batches so that the ingredients retain their moisture and crispness. This recipe uses canned tuna and so allows you to enjoy this Oriental dish at any time of the year.

WHOLE FISH BAKED IN PAPER

Oven temperature
180°C, 350°F, Gas 4

Cooking fish in paper prevents it from drying out and nearly all types of fish are suitable to cook this way. The fish is cooked when the paper browns and puffs up. The best part of cooking fish in this way is when you open the parcel and release the rich aroma that has formed during cooking. The French call this method of cooking *en papillote*.

1 tablespoon olive oil
4 large zucchini (courgettes), cut into strips
2 red peppers, cut into strips
rind from $1/2$ lemon, cut into strips
4 small whole fish, such as bream, sea perch, snapper or pompano, cleaned and scaled
2 tablespoons lemon juice

1   Heat oil in a large frying pan and stir-fry zucchini (courgettes), red peppers and lemon rind over a medium heat for 2-3 minutes. Remove pan from heat.

2   Cut four pieces of nonstick baking paper large enough to enclose each fish. Divide vegetable mixture between pieces of paper and top each with a fish. Sprinkle with lemon juice and fold baking paper around fish to enclose. Seal edges by rolling together tightly. Bake for 30 minutes or until flesh flakes when tested with a fork.

Serves 4

PAN-FRIED WHITING FILLETS

8 x 60 g/2 oz whiting fillets or 4 x
125 g/4 oz other firm white fish fillets
³/4 cup/90 g/3 oz flour
2 eggs, beaten
1 cup/125 g/4 oz dried breadcrumbs
60 g/2 oz butter

1   Dredge fillets in flour, then dip in egg and roll in breadcrumbs. Place fillets on a plate lined with plastic food wrap and refrigerate for 15 minutes or until ready to cook.

2   Melt butter in a large frying pan and cook fillets over a medium heat for 3-5 minutes each side or until flesh flakes when tested with fork. Serve immediately.

Serves 4

These fillets are delicious served with a bean salad made of cooked green beans, cooked chickpeas, cherry tomatoes, basil and thin strips of orange rind, tossed in a citrus dressing. To make the dressing, place 3 tablespoons olive oil, 1 crushed clove garlic, 1 tablespoon lime juice, 1 tablespoon lemon juice and 3 tablespoons orange juice in a screwtop jar and shake well to combine.

SEAFOOD LASAGNE

Oven temperature
180°C, 350°F, Gas 4

2 tablespoons olive oil
1 leek, white part only, sliced
440 g/14 oz canned tomatoes, undrained
and mashed
2 tablespoons tomato paste (purée)
500 g/1 lb uncooked prawns, shelled,
deveined and chopped
250 g/8 oz firm white fish fillets, cut
into pieces
freshly ground black pepper
15 spinach lasagne sheets
³/4 cup/90 g/3 oz grated mozzarella
cheese

1   Heat oil in a large frying pan and cook leek over a medium heat for 5 minutes or until it softens. Stir in tomatoes and tomato paste (purée) and bring to the boil. Reduce heat and simmer, uncovered, for 15 minutes or until sauce reduces and thickens slightly.

2   Add prawns and fish, cover and cook for 3-4 minutes longer. Season to taste with black pepper.

3   Cook lasagne in boiling water in a large saucepan following packet directions. Drain and place in a bowl of cold water.

4   Just prior to assembling, drain lasagne sheets. Spread one-third of the sauce over the base of a deep-sided ovenproof dish and top with half the lasagne sheets. Repeat layers, ending with a layer of sauce. Sprinkle with cheese and bake for 40 minutes.

Lasagne is a great dish when you need to feed a crowd. This recipe can easily be increased to serve 8; simply use a slightly larger dish and a little more seafood. Accompany with a tossed green salad or a sauté of mixed vegetables for a complete meal.

Serves 6

SCALLOPS WITH CHILLI AND LIME

185 g/6 oz green beans, cut into
5 cm/2 in lengths
185 g/6 oz snow peas (mangetout)
¹/₄ cup/60 mL/2 fl oz dry white wine
500 g/1 lb scallops

LIME DRESSING
3 tablespoons olive oil
2 tablespoons lime juice
2 tablespoons red wine vinegar
1 teaspoon chilli paste (sambal oelek)
1 tablespoon finely chopped fresh dill
freshly ground black pepper

1 Boil, steam or microwave beans and snow peas (mangetout) until just tender, Drain and refresh under cold running water. Drain again and set aside.

2 Place wine in a saucepan and bring to the boil. Add scallops and cook for 3 minutes or until scallops just turn opaque. Using a slotted spoon remove scallops and set aside.

3 To make dressing, place oil, lime juice, vinegar, chilli paste (sambal oelek), dill and black pepper to taste in a screwtop jar and shake well to combine.

4 Arrange beans, snow peas (mangetout) and scallops on a serving platter or individual plates and spoon dressing over.

Serves 4

Scallops require very little cooking and will become tough if overcooked. Fresh scallops will keep in an airtight container in the refrigerator for up to 3 days or can be frozen for up to 3 months.

SNAPPER WITH ARTICHOKE STUFFING

Oven temperature
180°C, 350°F, Gas 4

This could also be cooked on the barbecue. Cut two pieces of aluminium foil large enough to enclose each fish. Place a fish on each piece of foil, spoon wine mixture over fish and wrap foil around fish. Place on a preheated barbecue and cook for 20-30 minutes or until flesh flakes when tested with a fork.

2 whole small snapper, red mullet, bream or black sea bass, cleaned and scaled
2 tablespoons lemon juice
3 tablespoons lime juice
^{1}/4 cup/60 mL/2 fl oz dry white wine

ARTICHOKE STUFFING
30 g/1 oz butter
1 onion, chopped
2 cloves garlic, crushed
^{1}/2 red pepper, chopped
440 g/14 oz canned artichoke hearts, drained and chopped
2 tablespoons lime juice
1 tablespoon chopped fresh parsley
30 g/1 oz dried breadcrumbs
freshly ground black pepper

1   To make stuffing, melt butter in a frying pan and cook onion, garlic and red pepper over a medium heat for 5 minutes or until onion is soft. Transfer onion mixture to a bowl, add artichokes, lime juice, parsley, breadcrumbs and black pepper to taste. Mix well to combine.

2   Fill cavity of each fish with stuffing and secure with wooden toothpicks. Place fish in a lightly greased shallow ovenproof dish.

3   Place lemon juice, lime juice and wine in a bowl and mix to combine. Pour wine mixture over fish and bake, basting frequently, for 30-40 minutes or until flesh flakes when tested with a fork.

Serves 2

TUNA WITH YOGURT SAUCE

4 x 185 g/6 oz tuna steaks
¹/₄ cup/60 mL/2 fl oz lemon juice

YOGURT SAUCE
¹/₂ cup/100 g/3¹/₂ oz natural yogurt
3 tablespoons mayonnaise
1 tablespoon lime juice
¹/₄ cucumber, grated
125 g/4 oz seedless green grapes
freshly ground black pepper

1   To make sauce, place yogurt, mayonnaise, lime juice, cucumber, grapes and black pepper to taste in a bowl and mix well to combine.

2   Brush tuna with lemon juice and cook under a preheated grill for 3-4 minutes each side or until cooked to your liking. Serve tuna with Yogurt Sauce.

Serves 4

There are many species of tuna. The family includes marlin and swordfish, with mackerel being a close relative. All these fish are classed as oily and so have high levels of Omega-3 fatty acids. The flesh of these fish is firm and close-grained and ranges in colour from the white of swordfish to the deep red of bonito tuna. As a general guide, the lighter the flesh the more delicate the flavour.

Right: Lime-battered Seafood
Below: Tuna Fingers

TUNA FINGERS

Oven temperature
200°C, 400°F, Gas 6

220 g/7 oz canned tuna, drained
and flaked
2 potatoes, cooked and mashed
2 tablespoons chopped fresh parsley
1 tablespoon soy sauce
1 tablespoon chutney
freshly ground black pepper
1 egg, lightly beaten
1 cup/60 g/2 oz wholemeal breadcrumbs,
made from stale bread

1 Place tuna, potatoes, parsley, soy sauce, chutney and black pepper to taste in a bowl and mix to combine, gradually add egg to form a moist but not too soft mixture.

2 Divide mixture into ten portions and shape each portion into a 1 cm/¹/₂ in thick finger. Coat fingers in breadcrumbs, place on a plate lined with plastic food wrap, cover and refrigerate for 20 minutes.

3 Place fingers in a lightly oiled, shallow ovenproof dish and bake for 15-20 minutes or until fingers are golden and heated through.

Serves 4

These delicious homemade fish fingers can also be grilled or shallow-fried in oil until golden on both sides. Remember that frying will add kilojoules (calories).

LIME-BATTERED SEAFOOD

oil for deep-frying
8 large uncooked prawns, shelled and
deveined, tails left intact
60 g/2 oz calamari (squid) rings
4 x 90 g/3 oz firm white fish fillets

LIME BATTER
$1^1/2$ cups/185 g/6 oz flour, sifted
$1/2$ cup/125 mL/4 fl oz lime juice
1 cup/250 mL/8 fl oz soda water
2 teaspoons finely grated lime rind

CORIANDER MAYONNAISE
3 egg yolks
2 tablespoons lemon juice
$1/4$ teaspoon dry mustard
1 cup/250 mL/8 fl oz vegetable oil
1 tablespoon finely chopped
fresh coriander
freshly ground black pepper

1   To make batter, place flour in a bowl and gradually stir in lime juice and soda water. Mix well to combine, then stir in lime rind. Set aside.

2   To make mayonnaise, place egg yolks, lemon juice and mustard in a food processor or blender and process to combine. With machine running, slowly pour in oil and process until mixture thickens. Stir in coriander and season to taste with black pepper.

3   Heat oil in a large deep saucepan. Dip prawns, calamari (squid) rings and fish fillets in batter. Drain off excess batter and cook a few at a time in hot oil, until golden. Remove from pan and drain on absorbent kitchen paper. Serve with mayonnaise for dipping.

Serves 4

Never before have fish and chips been this good. Make your own chips and no one will be able to resist.
When heating oil for deep-frying, check the temperature by dropping a cube of bread into the hot oil. The oil is the right temperature when it will brown the bread cube in 50 seconds.

SALMON MORNAY

Oven temperature
180°C, 350°F, Gas 4

Fish can be a good source of bone-building calcium, an essential mineral mainly derived from milk. The edible bones in canned salmon and of tiny fish such as whitebait and sardines can be consumed with the flesh and provide substantial amounts of calcium.

$^1/_2$ cup/100 g/3$^1/_2$ oz rice
1 onion, chopped
1 egg, beaten
15 g/$^1/_2$ oz butter, melted
440 g/14 oz canned pink salmon,
drained, liquid reserved and flesh flaked
$^1/_4$ cup/15 g/$^1/_2$ oz breadcrumbs, made
from stale bread
30 g/1 oz grated tasty cheese
(mature Cheddar)

CURRY SAUCE
2 cups/500 mL/16 fl oz milk
3 tablespoons cornflour
1 teaspoon curry powder
1 teaspoon dry mustard
1 teaspoon paprika
2 tablespoons chopped fresh parsley
1 tablespoon lemon juice
1 egg, beaten
30 g/1 oz grated tasty cheese
(mature Cheddar)
freshly ground black pepper

1   Cook rice following packet directions. Place rice, onion, egg and melted butter in a bowl and mix to combine. Spread rice mixture over the base of an 18 x 28 cm/7 x 11 in ovenproof dish. Top rice mixture with salmon.

2   To make sauce, place milk, cornflour, curry powder, mustard and paprika in a saucepan and mix well to combine. Cook sauce over a medium heat, stirring constantly, for 5-6 minutes or until sauce boils and thickens. Stir in reserved salmon liquid, parsley, lemon juice, egg, cheese and black pepper to taste. Pour sauce over salmon.

3   Combine breadcrumbs and cheese and sprinkle over sauce. Bake for 40 minutes or until heated through and top is golden.

Serves 4

BARBECUED SKEWERED PRAWNS

When storing prawns, leave them in their shell. The shell acts as a natural insulator and helps retain moisture and flavour. Cooked prawns should be stored in the refrigerator in an airtight container or plastic food bag for no longer than 3 days. Uncooked prawns are best stored in water in an airtight container for up to 3 days. The water prevents oxidation.

500 g/1 lb large uncooked prawns,
shelled and deveined, tails left intact
2 teaspoons sesame oil
1 tablespoon soy sauce
1 tablespoon vegetable oil
1 teaspoon honey
1 clove garlic, crushed
freshly ground black pepper

1   Thread prawns onto oiled bamboo skewers.

2   Place sesame oil, soy sauce, vegetable oil, honey, garlic and black pepper to taste in a small bowl and whisk to combine. Brush prawns with oil mixture and cook under a preheated grill or on a preheated barbecue, brushing frequently with oil mixture, for 3-4 minutes each side or until prawns change colour and are cooked.

Serves 4

Salmon Mornay,
Barbecued Skewered Prawns

SNACKS

*Smoked salmon, and canned salmon and tuna
are the basis of many snacks and quick meals. In this
chapter you will find a variety of recipes that take only minutes
to create. The Egg and Salmon Sandwiches are perfect for
a special brunch or supper, while the Salmon Salad
Roll-Ups are great in a packed lunch.*

Smoked Salmon Bagels

SMOKED SALMON BAGELS

155 g/5 oz cream cheese
4 tablespoons sour cream
1 small onion, finely chopped
2 tablespoons chopped fresh parsley
1 tablespoon chopped capers
2 tablespoons lemon juice
freshly ground black pepper
8 bagels, split
1 bunch/250 g/8 oz watercress
250 g/8 oz sliced smoked salmon

1   Place cream cheese and sour cream in a small bowl and beat to combine. Stir in onion, parsley, capers, lemon juice and black pepper to taste.

2   Spread top half of each bagel with cream cheese mixture. Place watercress and salmon on each bottom half then cover with top half of bagel.

Makes 8

A bagel is a traditional Jewish roll. It is ring-shaped and is cooked twice. Cooking involves boiling first, for about 15 seconds, then the bagel is baked.

VEGETABLE AND SALMON SOUFFLES

$^1/_2$ cup/125 g/4 oz sour cream or natural yogurt
1 teaspoon chilli sauce
220 g/7 oz canned pink salmon, drained and flaked
2 eggs, separated
freshly ground black pepper
2 large zucchini (courgettes), grated

1   Place sour cream or yogurt, chilli sauce, salmon, egg yolks and black pepper to taste in a food processor or blender and process to combine. Stir in zucchini (courgettes).

2   Place egg whites in a bowl and beat until stiff peaks form. Fold egg whites into salmon mixture. Spoon soufflé mixture into four $1^1/_2$ cup/375 mL/12 fl oz capacity soufflé dishes and bake for 25 minutes or until soufflés are puffed and golden.

Serves 4

Oven temperature
200°C, 400°F, Gas 6

Mostly sold vacuum-packed, smoked salmon will keep in the refrigerator for about 10 days once opened. It also keeps well in the freezer. Smoked salmon should be pink-orange in colour, moist and with a mild smoky smell and delicate flavour.

'Fish is an important source of protein and contains many important minerals such as magnesium, iron, iodine and selenium.'

SEAFOOD KEBABS

8 scallops
2 x 125 g/4 oz firm white fish fillets,
cut into eight squares
8 cooked prawns, shelled and deveined

BASIL AND CHIVE BUTTER
125 g/4 oz butter, softened
2 tablespoons chopped fresh basil
2 tablespoons snipped fresh chives
1 tablespoon lemon juice
freshly ground black pepper

1 To make Basil and Chive Butter, place butter, basil, chives, lemon juice and black pepper to taste in a bowl and beat to combine.

2 Thread a scallop, a piece of fish and a prawn onto a lightly oiled bamboo skewer. Repeat with remaining seafood to make eight kebabs. Spread each kebab with a little butter and cook under a preheated grill, basting frequently for 3-4 minutes each side or until scallops and fish are cooked.

Serves 4

Remember to soak bamboo skewers in cold water for an hour or so before threading with food. This prevents them from splintering and burning during cooking. Lightly oil the skewers after soaking, this prevents the food from sticking and makes it easy to remove when eating.

SALMON SALAD ROLL-UPS

250 g/8 oz cream cheese
2 tablespoons snipped fresh chives
2 tablespoons lemon juice
freshly ground black pepper
4 pitta bread rounds
shredded lettuce
1/4 red pepper, sliced
1/4 green pepper, sliced
1 onion, chopped
440 g/14 oz canned pink salmon,
drained and flaked

1 Place cream cheese, chives, lemon juice and black pepper to taste in a bowl and beat to combine.

2 Spread each pitta bread with cream cheese mixture, then top with lettuce, red and green pepper, onion and salmon. Roll up tightly, secure with wooden toothpicks and serve immediately or wrap in plastic food wrap for a packed lunch.

Serves 4

Weight watchers might like to make these roll-ups using low-fat cottage or ricotta cheese instead of cream cheese.

'Fatty fish, such as tuna, salmon, sardines, herring and mackerel, have the highest levels of Omega-3.'

Seafood Kebabs,
Vegetable and Salmon Soufflés,
Salmon Salad Roll-ups

Right: Egg and Salmon Sandwiches
Below: Salmon Croquettes

SALMON CROQUETTES

3 large potatoes, cooked and mashed
1 onion, grated
440 g/14 oz canned pink salmon,
drained and flaked
1 teaspoon Dijon mustard
2 tablespoons mayonnaise
1 egg, beaten
freshly ground black pepper
200 g/6^1/$_2$ oz cheese-flavoured
biscuits, crushed
vegetable oil for deep-frying

These croquettes are great to have on hand for snacks and quick meals. After cooking, the croquettes can be frozen then all you need to do is reheat them in the oven at 180°C/350°F/Gas 4 for 15-20 minutes or until heated through.

1 Place potatoes, onion, salmon, mustard, mayonnaise, egg and black pepper to taste in a bowl and mix well to combine. Shape mixture into croquettes and roll in crushed biscuits to coat. Place croquettes on a plate lined with plastic food wrap and refrigerate for 15 minutes.

2 Heat oil in a large deep saucepan until a cube of bread dropped into it browns in 50 seconds. Add croquettes and cook over a medium heat for 4-5 minutes or until golden. Drain on absorbent kitchen paper and serve immediately.

Serves 4

EGG AND SALMON SANDWICHES

8 eggs
1/4 cup/60 mL/2 fl oz cream (double)
1 tablespoon snipped fresh chives
freshly ground black pepper
60 g/2 oz butter
4 slices bread
4 slices smoked salmon

1   Place eggs, cream, chives and black pepper to taste in a bowl and whisk to combine. Melt butter in a saucepan, add egg mixture and cook over a low heat, stirring gently, until egg mixture is set but still creamy.

2   Top each slice of bread with a slice of salmon, then with scrambled eggs. Serve immediately.

Serves 4

Keep this rather rich dish for a special brunch or supper dish. In place of the bread you might like to use a split bagel or a split, toasted English muffin.

SALADS

As a main meal or as a starter, a seafood salad is always welcome. In this chapter you will find exciting recipes for salads, such as Mussel and Potato Salad, Fresh Tuna Salad and Warm Seafood Salad. Whichever one you choose, you can be sure that it will not only taste good but it will also be good for you.

Prawn and Chilli Salad

Prawn and Chilli Salad

3/4 cup/185 mL/6 fl oz sweet white wine
1 tablespoon lemon juice
1 tablespoon lime juice
1 teaspoon sugar
1 teaspoon chilli paste (sambal oelek)
1 teaspoon chopped fresh coriander
freshly ground black pepper
315 g/10 oz scallops, cleaned
315 g/10 oz uncooked large prawns,
shelled and deveined, tails left intact
90 g/3 oz snow peas (mangetout)
2 tablespoons vegetable oil
1 tablespoon chopped fresh parsley

1   Place wine, lemon juice, lime juice, sugar, chilli paste (sambal oelek), coriander and black pepper to taste in a saucepan and bring to the boil over a medium heat.

2   Reduce heat to simmering, add scallops and prawns and cook for 2 minutes or until scallops are opaque and prawns just change colour. Using a slotted spoon remove scallops and prawns and place in a bowl.

3   Add snow peas (mangetout) to wine mixture and cook for 1 minute. Using a slotted spoon remove snow peas (mangetout) and add to bowl with scallops and prawns. Reserve cooking liquid.

4   Place oil, parsley and 4 tablespoons cooking liquid in a bowl and whisk to combine. Spoon over seafood mixture and toss to combine. Cover and chill for 2-3 hours before serving.

Serves 4 as a main course

Remember that many fish are seasonal and, just like fresh fruit and vegetables, those in season are usually the best quality and the most reasonably priced. Many recipes using fish are interchangeable so never be afraid to try a different type if the one stated in the recipe is unavailable or expensive.

Warm Seafood Salad

1/2 bunch/125 g/4 oz watercress, broken
into sprigs
1 lettuce, leaves separated
1 tablespoon olive oil
1 onion, sliced
1 clove garlic, crushed
315 g/10 oz scallops, cleaned
250 g/8 oz uncooked prawns, shelled
and deveined
250 g/8 oz firm white fish fillets, cut
into 2.5 cm/1 in squares
freshly ground black pepper

LIME DRESSING
1/2 cup/125 mL/4 fl oz lime juice
1 tablespoon olive oil
1 tablespoon finely chopped fresh dill

Serves 6 as a light meal

1   Make a bed of watercress sprigs and lettuce leaves on a large serving platter or on individual plates.

2   Heat oil in a large frying pan and cook onion and garlic over a medium heat for 4-5 minutes or until onion is soft. Add scallops, prawns and fish and cook, stirring, for 5-6 minutes or until prawns change colour, scallops are opaque and fish is cooked. Season to taste with black pepper. Place fish mixture on watercress and lettuce bed.

3   To make dressing, place lime juice, oil, dill and black pepper to taste in a screwtop jar and shake well to combine. Spoon dressing over fish mixture and serve immediately.

At around 793 kilojoules (189 Calories) this warm seafood salad makes a marvellous 'lite' meal for any weight watcher.

FRESH TUNA SALAD

250 g/1 lb green beans
2 teaspoons chopped capers
2 tablespoons vegetable oil
500 g/1 lb tuna steaks, cut into chunks
1 lettuce, leaves separated
440 g/14 oz canned cannellini or lima
beans, drained and rinsed
1 red pepper, roasted, skin removed,
sliced
1 red onion, thinly sliced
2 hard-boiled eggs, quartered
12 cherry tomatoes
12 large black olives

LIME DRESSING
3 tablespoons olive oil
2 tablespoons lime juice
freshly ground black pepper

1 Boil, steam or microwave beans until just tender. Drain and refresh under cold running water. Place beans and capers in a bowl and toss to combine.

2 Heat oil in a large frying pan and stir-fry tuna for 3-4 minutes or until just cooked.

3 Arrange green bean mixture, tuna, lettuce, cannellini or lima beans, red pepper, onion, eggs, tomatoes and olives attractively on a large serving platter.

4 To make dressing, place oil, lime juice and black pepper to taste in a screwtop jar and shake well to combine. Drizzle dressing over salad. Serve immediately.

Serves 6 as a main course

If tuna is unavailable you might like to use salmon or swordfish instead.

RAW FISH SALAD

440 g/14 oz firm white fish fillets, cut
into strips
$^1/_4$ cup/60 mL/2 fl oz lemon juice
3 tablespoons white wine vinegar
3 tablespoons white wine
2 cloves garlic, crushed
2 large carrots, cut into strips
250 g/8 oz asparagus spears, cut
into 3 cm/1$^1/_4$ in lengths
1 red pepper, chopped
1 tablespoon chopped fresh parsley
freshly ground black pepper

1   Place fish, lemon juice, vinegar, wine
and garlic in a bowl, toss to combine,
cover and refrigerate for 2 hours.

2   Boil, steam or microwave carrots and
asparagus separately until just tender.
Drain and refresh under cold running
water.

3   Drain fish and place in a salad bowl.
Add carrots, asparagus, red pepper, parsley
and black pepper to taste and toss to
combine.

Serves 4 as a main course

There are many variations on
uncooked fish salad,
however they all rely on an
acid ingredient – in this
recipe, lemon juice – to
'cook' the fish as it marinates,
making it firm and white.

53

MUSSEL AND POTATO SALAD

1 tablespoon olive oil
1 onion, chopped
1 clove garlic, crushed
$^1/_2$ cup/125 mL/4 fl oz dry white wine
1 tablespoon lemon juice
2 tablespoons sugar
1 teaspoon oyster sauce
2 tablespoons red wine vinegar
24 mussels, cooked, meat removed
and shells discarded
500 g/1 lb baby potatoes, cooked
and halved
1 teaspoon chopped fresh parsley
1 red pepper, roasted, peeled and cut
into strips
freshly ground black pepper

For a complete meal, serve this substantial main course with a salad of mixed lettuces and herbs.

1   Heat oil in a large frying pan and cook onion and garlic over a medium heat for 2 minutes. Add wine, lemon juice, sugar, oyster sauce and vinegar and bring to the boil. Reduce heat and simmer until reduced by half.

2   Add mussels and potatoes to pan and cook, stirring, for 4-5 minutes or until heated through. Stir in parsley, red pepper and black pepper to taste. Serve warm or at room temperature.

Serves 4 as a main course

Left: Herbed Seafood Salad
Far left: Mussel and Potato Salad

HERBED SEAFOOD SALAD

24 scallops, cooked
24 large cooked prawns, shelled and
deveined, tails left intact
1 fresh red chilli, seeded and
finely sliced
$^1/_4$ green pepper, cut into strips
30 g/1 oz green olives, pitted and halved
2 tablespoons chopped fresh coriander
$^1/_4$ cup/60 mL/2 fl oz safflower oil
freshly ground black pepper

ORANGE MARINADE
4 tablespoons vinegar
$^1/_4$ cup/60 mL/2 fl oz lime or
lemon juice
$^1/_4$ cup/60 mL/2 fl oz orange juice
1 clove garlic, crushed

1 To make marinade, place vinegar, lime or lemon juice, orange juice and garlic in a bowl and whisk to combine. Add scallops and prawns and toss to coat. Cover and refrigerate for 2 hours.

2 Drain seafood and reserve marinade. Add chilli, green pepper, olives and coriander to seafood mixture and toss well to combine.

3 Place reserved marinade, oil and black pepper to taste in a screwtop jar and shake well to combine. Just prior to serving, drizzle dressing over salad.

Serves 6 as a main course

To cook scallops, place 1 cup/250 mL/8 fl oz water, wine or fish stock in a saucepan and bring to simmering, add scallops and cook for 1-2 minutes or until they are opaque.

CELEBRATIONS

*Lobster Salad or a mixed seafood platter
makes the perfect meal for a special occasion. If serving a
large crowd, just add oysters, mussels or other favourite seafood
dishes to the platter. You will find many ideas in this book,
especially in the Starters chapter.*

Lobster Salad

Marinated Fish Salad

Spicy Grilled Octopus

Prawns with Curry Dip

Lobster Salad

LOBSTER SALAD

2 lobster tails or crayfish, cooked
and shells removed
1 radicchio, leaves separated
1 lettuce, leaves separated
100 g/3^{1}/$_{2}$ oz snow pea sprouts
or watercress
1 orange, segmented
250 g/8 oz strawberries

RASPBERRY DRESSING
125 g/4 oz fresh or frozen raspberries
2 tablespoons raspberry vinegar
2 tablespoons vegetable oil
1 teaspoon chopped fresh mint
1 tablespoon sugar

1   Cut lobster tails into 1 cm/^{1}/$_{2}$ in thick medallions and set aside.

2   Arrange radicchio and lettuce leaves, sprouts or watercress, orange segments, strawberries and lobster attractively on a serving platter. Cover and refrigerate.

3   To make dressing, place raspberries in a food processor or blender and process until puréed. Push purée through a sieve to remove seeds. Place raspberry purée, vinegar, oil, mint and sugar in a small bowl and mix to combine. Drizzle dressing over salad and serve immediately.

Serves 4 as a main course

To cook lobster, place dead lobster in a saucepan of cold water, bring slowly to the boil and boil, allowing 8 minutes per 500 g/1 lb of lobster. To kill a live lobster, either drown it in fresh water or freeze it.

MARINATED FISH SALAD

4 tablespoons white wine vinegar
2 tablespoons lemon juice
1 tablespoon sugar
500 g/1 lb firm white fish fillets, cut
into large pieces
1 cucumber, thinly sliced
1 red pepper, chopped
4 spring onions, chopped
250 g/8 oz cherry tomatoes, halved

LEMON AND MINT DRESSING
2 tablespoons white wine vinegar
2 tablespoons lemon juice
4 tablespoons olive oil
1 tablespoon sugar
1 tablespoon finely chopped fresh mint
freshly ground black pepper

1   Place vinegar, lemon juice and sugar in a bowl and whisk to combine. Set aside.

2   Bring a large saucepan of water to simmering, add fish and cook for 2-3 minutes or until fish turns opaque. Using a slotted spoon remove fish and add to vinegar mixture. Toss to combine, cover and refrigerate for 30 minutes.

3   To make dressing, place vinegar, lemon juice, oil, sugar, mint and black pepper to taste in a screwtop jar and shake well to combine.

4   Drain fish and place in a salad bowl. Add cucumber, red pepper, spring onions, tomatoes and dressing and toss to combine. Serve immediately.

Serves 6 as a main course

This salad looks great served on a bed of torn lettuce leaves or in lettuce or radicchio cups.

SPICY GRILLED OCTOPUS

1.5 kg/3 lb baby octopus

SPICY MARINADE
1/4 cup/60 mL/2 fl oz tomato sauce
3 teaspoons malt vinegar
3 teaspoons soy sauce
2 tablespoons honey
2 teaspoons oil
2 cloves garlic, crushed
2 teaspoons grated fresh ginger
1-2 teaspoons hot chilli sauce

1 Remove heads from octopus by cutting just below the eyes. Remove beaks and wash octopus well. Bring a large saucepan of water to simmering and cook octopus for 2 minutes or until opaque. Drain and refresh under cold running water.

2 To make marinade, place tomato sauce, vinegar, soy sauce, honey, oil, garlic, ginger and chilli sauce in a bowl and mix to combine. Add octopus and toss to coat. Cover and refrigerate for 8 hours.

3 Drain octopus and cook under a preheated grill or on a preheated barbecue for 3-4 minutes. Serve immediately.

Serves 6

Fresh octopus will keep in the refrigerator for up to 2 days. Clean it before storing and wrap in plastic food wrap. Octopus can also be frozen for up to 3 months.

PRAWNS WITH CURRY DIP

1.5 kg/3 lb cooked large prawns, shelled and deveined, tails left intact

CURRY DIP
1 tablespoon oil
2 cloves garlic, crushed
1 1/2 tablespoons curry powder
1 tablespoon sugar
1/2 cup/125 mL/4 fl oz chicken stock
1 cup/250 mL/8 fl oz coconut milk
2 tablespoons lemon juice
freshly ground black pepper

To make dip, heat oil in a saucepan and cook garlic, curry powder and sugar over a medium heat for 1 minute. Stir in stock, coconut milk and lemon juice and bring to the boil. Reduce heat and simmer for 5 minutes or until dip thickens slightly and reduces. Season to taste with black pepper. Serve with prawns.

Serves 6

To cook raw prawns, bring a large saucepan of water to the boil, add the prawns and cook for 3-5 minutes or until they change colour. Take care not to overcook them or they will be tough.

*Marinated Fish Salad,
Spicy Grilled Octopus,
Prawns with Curry Dip*

WHOLE FISH WITH ORANGE BUTTER

1 kg/2 lb whole small fish, such as
snapper or bream, cleaned and scaled
60 g/2 oz butter
4 spring onions, chopped
1 clove garlic, crushed
1 orange, segmented
2 tablespoons chopped fresh parsley
1 cup/60 g/2 oz breadcrumbs, made
from stale bread
freshly ground black pepper

ORANGE BUTTER
125 g/4 oz butter, softened
3 teaspoons finely grated orange rind
1 tablespoon orange juice
2 teaspoons tomato sauce

This dish is also delicious
baked in the oven. Prepare
as described in the recipe,
then cook at 180°C/350°F/
Gas 4 for 30-35 minutes or
until flesh flakes when tested
with a fork.

1 Preheat barbecue to a medium heat.
Run a knife inside fish across bones,
starting from head and working down to
the tail to remove bones. Take care not to
cut through back. Turn fish and repeat
with other side. Cut centre bone at both
ends and gently lift out.

2 Melt butter in a large frying pan and
cook spring onions and garlic for 1-2
minutes. Remove pan from heat and stir
in orange segments, parsley, breadcrumbs
and black pepper to taste. Fill cavity of
each fish with breadcrumb mixture. Close
cavity and secure with wooden
toothpicks.

3 Cut a piece of aluminium foil large
enough to completely enclose the fish.
Lightly grease foil and place fish in
centre. Fold foil over fish to enclose
completely and seal by rolling edges
together. Cook fish on preheated
barbecue grill, turning several times for
25-30 minutes or until flesh flakes when
tested with a fork.

4 To make Orange Butter, place butter,
orange rind, orange juice, tomato sauce
and black pepper to taste in a bowl and
mix to combine. Place butter mixture on
a piece of aluminium foil and form into a
sausage shape. Wrap foil around butter
and refrigerate until firm. Cut into slices
and serve with fish.

Serves 4

Keep the bones and
trimmings of fish to make fish
stock; see recipe later in this
section. If you do not have
sufficient bones and
trimmings to make a good
size batch of stock, freeze
them and add to them until
you do have enough.
Remember that you can
also freeze prawn, lobster
and crab shells to be used
for stock.

Whole Fish with Orange Butter

PINK AND WHITE FISH MOSAIC

The sauce is also delicious made with sorrel in place of the spinach.

4 large firm white fish fillets, skin and bones removed
2 tablespoons lemon juice
freshly ground white pepper
16 large spinach leaves, stalks removed and leaves blanched
2 salmon fillets, skin and bones removed

SPINACH SAUCE
45 g/1^1/2 oz butter
2 spring onions, chopped
1 clove garlic, crushed
2 fresh sage leaves
200 g/6^1/2 oz young spinach leaves
2 cups/500 mL/16 fl oz fish stock
1 bay leaf
^{1}/2 cup/125 mL/4 fl oz dry white wine
1 cup/250 mL/8 fl oz cream (double)
freshly ground black pepper

These attractive fish squares can be easily cooked in the microwave. To cook in the microwave, place the prepared fish squares on a piece of nonstick baking paper rather than the aluminium foil, place in a shallow microwave-safe dish, cover and cook on HIGH (100%) for 4-5 minutes or until fish is cooked.

1   Cut each white fish fillet lengthwise into four strips, each measuring 15 x 2 cm/ 6 x ^{3}/4 in (this will give you sixteen strips). Sprinkle with 1 tablespoon lemon juice and season to taste with white pepper. Wrap each strip in blanched spinach leaves and set aside.

Serves 4

2   Cut salmon fillets crosswise into sixteen strips the same size as the white fish strips. Sprinkle with remaining lemon juice and season to taste with white pepper.

3   Weave four strips of each fish into a square to form a chequerboard pattern on each piece of foil. Trim ends if necessary. Place a wire rack and 2.5 cm/1 in water in a large frying pan, cover and bring to the boil. Place fish on wire rack and steam for 6-8 minutes or until fish is cooked.

4   To make sauce, melt half the butter in a saucepan and cook spring onions, garlic and sage for 2 minutes. Add spinach and cook over a low heat for 5 minutes longer or until spinach leaves are wilted. Add stock, bay leaf and wine, bring to the boil and boil until mixture reduces by half. Remove bay leaf.

5   Place sauce in a food processor or blender and process until smooth. Pass through a fine sieve into a clean saucepan. Stir in cream and cook over a low heat for 5 minutes. Whisk in small pieces of remaining butter. Season to taste with black pepper and set aside and keep warm. Serve fish squares with sauce.

Pink and White Fish Mosaic

TUNA AND PRAWN SUSHI

12 large cooked prawns, shelled,
deveined, tails left intact
2 teaspoons wasabi powder
125 g/4 oz sashimi (fresh) tuna
1 sheet nori (seaweed), cut into
strips (optional)
soy sauce

SUSHI RICE
500 g/1 lb short grain rice
2¹/₂ cups/600 mL/1 pt water
2 tablespoons sweet sake or sherry
4 tablespoons rice vinegar
2 tablespoons sugar
¹/₂ teaspoon salt

Strips of spring onion can be used in place of the nori (seaweed) if you wish.

1 For the rice, wash rice several times in cold water and set aside to drain for 30 minutes. Place rice and water in a large saucepan and bring to the boil, cover and cook, without stirring, over a low heat for 15 minutes. Remove pan from heat and set aside for 10 minutes.

2 Place sake or sherry, vinegar, sugar and salt in a small saucepan and bring to the boil. Remove pan from heat and set aside to cool.

Wasabi is a very hot horseradish powder. It is available from Asian food stores.

3 Turn rice out into a large shallow dish, pour over vinegar mixture and toss gently until rice has cooled to room temperature. Take a tablespoon of rice in your hand and gently squeeze it to form a neat oval. Place on a serving platter and repeat with remaining rice to make 24 ovals.

4 Split prawns on the underside – taking care not to cut all the way through – and flatten them out. Mix wasabi powder with a few drops of water to make a smooth paste and dab a little on each rice oval. Top twelve rice ovals with prawns.

5 Cut tuna into twelve 2 x 4 cm/³/₄ x 1¹/₂ in strips each 5 mm/¹/₄ in thick. Top remaining rice ovals with tuna strips. Wrap a strip of nori (seaweed), if using, around each sushi. Serve sushi with soy sauce for dipping.

Makes 24

Tuna and Prawn Sushi

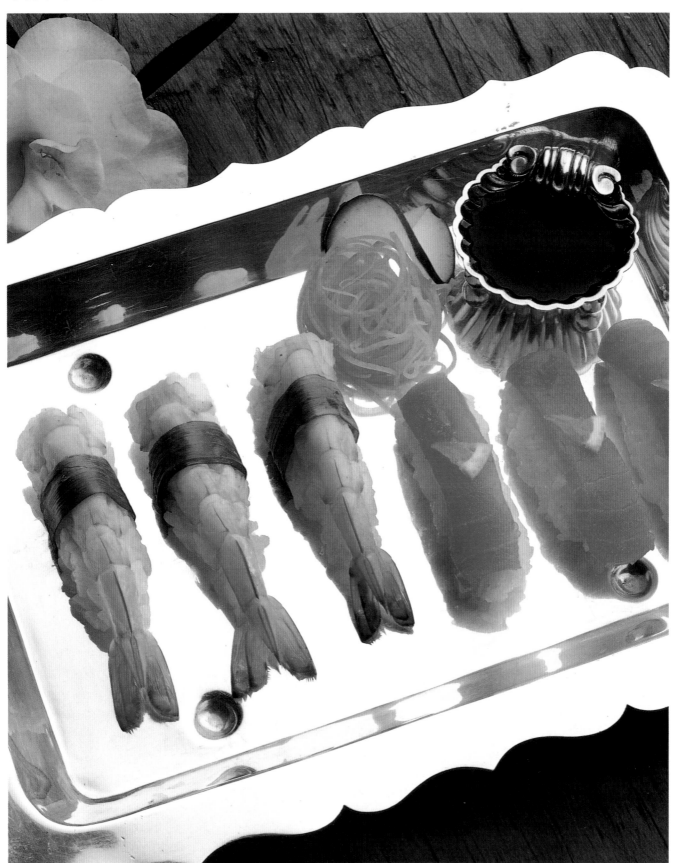

CLEANING AND PREPARING CALAMARI

Calamari (squid) can often be purchased already cleaned as hoods or tubes, or cut into rings. However, it is easy to clean and prepare; just follow these simple step-by-step instructions.

The method of crisscross cutting of calamari (squid) – known as 'honeycombing' – is used to tenderise it. It also gives an attractive appearance.

1 Pull tentacles from the calamari (squid), carefully taking with them the stomach and ink bag.

4 Cut hood in rings, or 'honeycomb'. To honeycomb calamari (squid), make a single cut down the length of the hood or body and open out. Using a sharp knife, cut parallel lines down the length of the calamari, taking care not to cut right through the flesh. Make more cuts in the opposite direction to form a diamond pattern. Cut each piece into 3 or 4 pieces.

2 Cut the beak, stomach and ink bag from the tentacles and discard. Wash tentacles well.

Calamari (squid) should always be cleaned before storing. It will keep in the refrigerator for up to 3 days or can be frozen for up to 3 months.

3 Wash 'hood' (body) and peel away skin.

CRISPY ALMOND CALAMARI

500 g/1 lb calamari (squid) tubes,
cleaned
$^{1}/_{2}$ cup/60 g/2 oz flour
freshly ground black pepper
2 eggs, lightly beaten
1 cup/125 g/4 oz dried breadcrumbs
60 g/2 oz finely chopped almonds
oil for deep-frying

1   Slice calamari (squid) into rings.

2   Combine flour and black pepper to taste on a shallow plate. Place eggs on a separate plate and combine breadcrumbs and almonds on a third plate.

3   Roll calamari (squid) rings in flour, then dip in egg and finally roll in breadcrumb mixture. Place on a baking tray lined with nonstick baking paper and refrigerate for 15 minutes or until ready to cook.

4   Heat oil in a large saucepan until a cube of bread dropped in, browns in 50 seconds. Cook calamari (squid) in batches for 1-2 minutes or until golden. Remove using a slotted spoon and drain on absorbent kitchen paper. Serve immediately.

Serves 4

If you find it difficult to remove the skin from the body of the calamari (squid), dip your fingers in a little salt – this helps you to get a firm grip on the calamari (squid) and so makes it easy to remove the skin.

Crispy Almond Calamari

STUFFED CALAMARI RINGS

4 large calamari (squid)
4 lettuce leaves
4 sheets nori (seaweed)
$^1/_2$ cup/125 mL/4 fl oz light soy sauce
$^1/_2$ cup/125 mL/4 fl oz water
3 tablespoons sugar

1 Clean and prepare calamari (squid) as previously described. Place lettuce leaves in a bowl, cover with boiling water, then drain.

As a general guide, allow 250 g/8 oz of raw calamari (squid) per serve when making quick-cooking dishes such as stir-fries and allow 500 g/1 lb per serve when braising or stewing. On longer cooking you will find that considerable shrinkage takes place, hence the larger quantity required.

2 Place one-quarter of the calamari (squid) tentacles on a lettuce leaf, wrap up tightly then enclose in a nori (seaweed)

sheet and seal by lightly wetting the edge. Repeat with remaining tentacles, lettuce leaves and nori (seaweed) sheets.

3 Insert tentacle parcels in calamari (squid) hoods and secure ends with a wooden toothpick.

4 Place soy sauce, water and sugar in a saucepan, bring to simmering, then add calamari (squid) parcels and simmer for 30-40 minutes or until calamari (squid) is tender. Using a slotted spoon remove calamari parcels, drain and refrigerate overnight. To serve, cut into slices.

Makes 36 slices

'The tentacles, body sac and ink of calamari (squid) are edible. The ink has a rich, fishy flavour and a popular Mediterranean dish is squid cooked in its ink.'

Stuffed Calamari Rings

SMOKED SALMON QUICHES

185 g/6 oz prepared puff pastry

SMOKED SALMON FILLING
6 eggs
1¹/₂ cups/375 mL/12 oz cream (double)
¹/₄ teaspoon ground nutmeg
freshly ground black pepper
125 g/4 oz smoked salmon, chopped
2 teaspoons chopped fresh dill

Oven temperature
200°C, 400°F, Gas 6

3 Divide salmon mixture between pastry cases and bake for 10-15 minutes or until quiches are puffed and golden.

These quiches can be made in advance, removed from the pans and stored in a covered container in the refrigerator. To reheat, place quiches on baking trays lined with nonstick baking paper and heat at 200°C/400°F/ Gas 6 for 5 minutes or until quiches are heated through.

1 Roll out pastry to 3 mm/¹/₈ in thick and cut out twenty-four pastry rounds using a 6 cm/2¹/₂ in pastry cutter. Press pastry rounds into shallow, greased patty pans (tartlet tins).

2 To make filling, place eggs, cream, nutmeg and black pepper to taste in a bowl and whisk to combine. Mix in salmon and dill.

Makes 24

'Smoked salmon should be pink-orange in colour, moist and with a mild smoky smell and delicate flavour.'

Smoked Salmon Quiches

CLEANING AND PREPARING PRAWNS

Shelling and deveining prawns is a somewhat time-consuming job. The method is the same for both raw and cooked prawns.

1   Break off head and remove shell. The tail can be left intact or removed, depending on how you intend to use the prawns. Using a small sharp knife, make a shallow cut along the back of the prawn and remove the black vein.

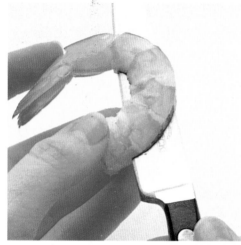

Butterflying prawns makes them attractive for presentation and is a great way of preparing prawns for cooking on the barbecue.

2   To butterfly a prawn, lay prawn on its side and, using a small sharp knife, slice through the back of the prawn, making sure the flesh at the tail and head ends is not severed.

Butterflied Prawn

3   Turn prawn over so the back is facing up and open out gently to form a butterfly shape. It may be necessary to gently press the flesh to flatten it slightly. You will find that the tail naturally curls into place.

FISH STOCK

fish bones, skin, trimmings and
seafood shells; the quantity and type
used is not important
500 g/1 lb white fish
1 onion, sliced
1 leek, sliced
1 carrot, sliced
2 tablespoons lemon juice
bouquet garni
8 cups/2 litres/3$^1/2$ pt water
1 teaspoon black peppercorns

Fish stock is even better if you can include the shells of lobster, prawns or crab.

1 Place fish bones, skin, trimmings, seafood shells, white fish, onion, leek, carrot, lemon juice, bouquet garni, water and peppercorns in a large saucepan and bring to the boil over a medium heat. Reduce heat and simmer, uncovered, for 25 minutes.

2 Skim surface of stock as required during cooking. Strain stock through a fine sieve and set aside to cool. Cover and store in the refrigerator for up to two days or freeze for up to 12 months.

Makes 5 cups/1.2 litres/2 pt

Rich Fish Stock: For a richer stock use 6 cups/1.5 litres/2$^1/2$ pt water and 2 cups/ 500 mL/16 fl oz dry white wine. After stock has simmered for 25 minutes, strain and return it to a clean pan. Bring to the boil, then reduce heat and simmer until reduced to two-thirds.

When making fish stock it is important that the cooking time is no longer than 25 minutes as the bones and trimmings become bitter and impart an unpleasant taste.

WHY EAT SEAFOOD?

Recent research shows that there are various reasons why we should eat seafood:

It is low in fat and so low in kilojoules (calories); it contains many essential vitamins and minerals; it is a good source of protein; it contains Omega-3 fatty acids which have been shown to help prevent heart disease; and – best of all – it makes a delicious meal.

For slimmers, seafood is the ideal meal. Did you know that 100 g/3^1/$_2$ oz of white fish such as cod, bream or snapper (cooked without fat) contains only 375 kJ (90 Cal) and that a dozen raw oysters has only 335 kJ (80 Cal)? Lobster, prawns, squid and octopus are also good choices for weight watchers, but remember all seafood should be cooked without fat for the full benefits to be appreciated.

Nutritionists and health professionals now recommend that we eat seafood at least three times a week.

BUYING FISH AND SHELLFISH

As a general rule, seafood should look fresh and have a pleasant sea smell. The following guide will assist you.

A GUIDE TO BUYING FISH AND SHELLFISH

	Look For	Watch Out For
Fillets	Fillets should be shiny and firm with a pleasant sea smell.	Fillets that are dull, soft, discoloured or 'ooze' water when touched indicate that the fish is past its best.
Whole Fish	Whole fish should have a pleasant sea smell and a bright lustre to the skin. Gills should be red and the eyes bright and bulging. When touched, the flesh should be firm and springy.	Dull-coloured fish with sunken eyes should be avoided at all costs.
Smoked Fish	Smoked fish should have a pleasant smoked smell and be dry.	Avoid smoked fish that is 'sweaty' or slimy with a rancid smell.
Lobster (cooked)	The limbs of lobster should be intact and the tails curled. Eyes should be bright and the lobster should feel heavy in proportion to its size.	Discoloration at the joints and missing or loose limbs indicate that the lobster is past its best.
Mussels (live)	The shells of live mussels should be tightly closed.	Open shells; this indicates the mussels are already dead.
Oysters	Oysters should be plump, and shiny with a natural creamy colour and clear liquid. They should have a pleasant sea smell and be free of shell particles.	Oysters with an 'off' smell should be avoided at all costs.
Prawns (cooked)	The flesh of cooked prawns should be firm and the shells tight. They should have a pleasant sea smell.	Avoid limp-looking prawns with black loose heads or legs.
Prawns (uncooked)	Uncooked prawns should have a firm body and a pleasant sea smell.	Uncooked prawns should show no sign of black.

FROZEN SEAFOOD

As with all food, if you plan to freeze seafood, it should be as fresh as possible.

❧ Remember that seafood has a shorter freezer life than meat or chicken, because of the high proportion of polyunsaturated fats in it.

❧ To retain the flavour of oily fish, dip it in a mixture of lemon juice and water before freezing. Use the juice of 1 large lemon to 2 cups/500 mL/16 fl oz of water.

❧ When freezing fish it is often recommended to ice glaze it. Ice glazing forms a coating of ice around the fish and acts as insulation. It is a good method of protecting large whole fish, which are difficult to wrap. Whole fish, fillets or cutlets can be ice glazed.

❧ To ice glaze, place the fish on a freezerproof tray lined with plastic food wrap and freeze, uncovered, using the fast-freeze control for $1^{1}/_{2}$-2 hours or until the fish is solid. Remove the fish from the freezer and dip in cold water then return to the freezer and freeze for 30 minutes or until a solid ice coating forms. Repeat this process two or three times or until a coating of ice about 5 mm/$^{1}/_{4}$ in thick has formed. Wrap fish for freezing and freeze as usual.

❧ Before freezing, prepare the fish or shellfish for use. For example, if you want to serve fillets of fish, it is best to fillet the fish before freezing.

❧ When buying frozen fish watch out for freezer burn; this indicates that the fish has been wrapped incorrectly for freezing and has dehydrated. Freezer burn appears as dry, white or brown patches on the flesh of the fish.

❧ Frozen seafood is best cooked directly from frozen. Just allow a little extra cooking time. Cooking seafood from frozen ensures that it holds its shape and retains its flavour and texture better. If you are going to batter or crumb fillets or stuff a whole fish, you will need to thaw them slightly.

❧ Fish fillets can be crumbed before freezing. Crumb as usual, then place on a freezerproof tray lined with plastic food wrap and freeze, uncovered, using the fast-freeze control for $1^{1}/_{2}$-2 hours or until fish is solid. Pack for freezing.

❧ Use the following guide for recommended freezing times to ensure that your frozen seafood stays at its best.

RECOMMENDED FREEZING TIMES FOR SEAFOOD	
Non-oily fish, such as bream, cod flounder, sole, snapper or John Dory	4-6 months
Oily fish, such as anchovy, mullet, salmon or tuna	3 months
Shellfish	3 months
Smoked fish	3 months
Oysters	6 weeks

FISH ALTERNATIVES

The types and names of fish vary from region to region and country to country. This brief guide gives you some suggested alternatives if a specified fish is unavailable.

Altantic Salmon	Salmon
Flounder	Sole
Gemfish	Sea Bream
Ling	Pike, Perch
Kingfish	Snapper, Ling, Jewfish
Ocean Perch	Sea Bass, Turbot
Ocean Trout	Salmon Trout
Orange Roughy	Sea Perch
Snapper	Sea Perch, Sea Bream

INDEX

UK COOKERY EDITOR
Katie Swallow

EDITORIAL
Food Editor: Rachel Blackmore
Editorial Assistant: Ella Martin
Editorial Coordinator: Margaret Kelly
Recipe Development: Sheryle Eastwood, Lucy Kelly, Donna Hay,
Anneka Mitchell, Penelope Peel, Belinda Warn, Loukie Werle
Credits: Recipes pages 11, 12, 13, 67 by June Budgen; page 73 by
Gordon Grimsdale © Merehurst Limited

COVER
Photography: Ashley Mackevicius
Styling: Wendy Berecry
Plate from Villeroy and Boch

PHOTOGRAPHY
Per Ericson, Ashley Mackevicius, Harm Mol, Yanto Noerianto,
Andy Payne, Warren Webb

STYLING
Wendy Berecry, Belinda Clayton, Rosemary De Santis, Carolyn
Fienberg, Jacqui Hing, Michelle Gorry

DESIGN AND PRODUCTION
Manager: Sheridan Carter
Layout: Lulu Dougherty
Finished Art: Stephen Joseph
Design: Frank Pithers

Published by J.B. Fairfax Press Pty Ltd
A.C.N. 003 738 430
Formatted by J.B. Fairfax Press Pty Ltd
Output by Adtype, Sydney
Printed in Italy by G. Canale & C. S.p.A. - Turin

Includes Index
1 86343 075 X (pbk)
1 85391 289 1

Distributed by J.B. Fairfax Press Ltd
9 Trinity Centre, Park Farm Estate
Wellingborough, Northants
Ph: (0933) 402330 Fax: (0933) 402234